SHARING YOUR FAITH

GROUP BIBLE STUDY

WRITTEN BY Jay T. Harvey

RELEVANCE
SERIES

CONTENTS

L1   Lesson 1   The Source for Sharing 5

L2   Lesson 2   Sharing by Listening.................................. 19

L3   Lesson 3   Sharing Your Story................................... 33

L4   Lesson 4   Sharing by Example 47

L5   Lesson 5   Sharing in the Struggle 59

L6   Lesson 6   Sharing from God's Word 71

The Warner Press *Relevance* Group Bible Studies provide intriguing examinations of topics using the whole of the Scriptures. The guides incorporate various stories and activities to introduce and apply the subject matter, with a Bible study component at the heart of each session. Our goal is to show life-long believers and those new to the faith how to know the Lord intimately while encouraging them to step out and join him in his work with miraculous results.

These flexible studies are ideal for any setting. We know that time is a valuable commodity in today's society, and that's why each book consists of five or six short lessons intended to meet the group's scheduling needs.

The Source for Sharing

Psalm 145; John 3:17

Main Point

In order to have the proper motivation for sharing our faith, we must get in touch with the source of our faith.

Background

Psalm 145 beautifully reveals God as our loving King, prompting us to tell of God's mighty acts from generation to generation. The psalm shares characteristics of God that warrant praise: the love, protection, favor, compassion, and redemption he bestows on those who love him. These verses put us in the right frame of mind for sharing our faith with others. John 3:17 reveals the heart behind God's sending of Jesus, speaking to God's love and the purpose for Jesus coming: "not…to condemn the world, but to save the world." This is key when sharing our faith. Jesus came for a very positive reason.

Sharing the Good Things

Why is it so easy to share with others all the exciting and positive things happening in our lives? You know how it goes; someone will approach you and say, "Wow, you look great. Have you lost weight?" Game on! You can hardly contain your excitement because someone noticed.

People get excited about things they are passionate about and that have had an impact on their lives. Most of us have friends who try something new all the time and promptly call up to let us know. "I've found the best diet!" they proclaim, or, "I bought that new exercise thingy they show on television and I'm going to get in shape just as soon as the holidays are over."

What areas of your life do you like to share with others? Why?

____

____

____

____

____

What areas of your life are you uncomfortable sharing about? Why? If you are not comfortable sharing about them here, you might mention things that people in general tend to be uncomfortable sharing about.

____

____

____

____

____

____

What goes into your thought process when sharing about certain areas
of your life with others? In other words, what determines whether or not
something is "worthy" of sharing?

____

____

____

____

____

I. **Read** Psalm 145:1–7.

Sharing our faith is important. Talking about our love for God is much easier to do when we are reminded of the greatness of God and his love for us. This psalm starts by exalting God as "King." Why is this a fitting title for God? From the passage and from your own experience and knowledge, why is God a good King?

____

____

____

____

What is important about praising God on a regular basis, even daily? What does it do for us? What does it do for God?

____

____

____

____

This psalm emphasizes sharing God's mighty acts with others. What are some of God's mighty acts that you would feel comfortable sharing with others?

____

____

____

II. Read Psalm 145:8–16.

What is the difference in being "slow to anger" and never becoming angry at all? What are some examples from "human" situations (family, work, etc.) you might give? In what ways and circumstances might anger be a good thing?

How does the fact of God's rule being eternal inspire us to praise him and tell others about him?

What if God were only trustworthy and faithful *most* of the time? How could this be worse than a God who was inconsistent in his actions and responses or who was never faithful at all?

III. Read Psalm 145:17–21.

What does it mean for God to be "near" to us? If the sense of this idea is not physical, how would you describe it?

What does it mean to "fear" God? If the sense of this idea is more than being afraid of punishment, how would you describe it?

How can creatures other than human beings praise the Lord?

How do these verses encourage you? Write down three characteristics about God you can count on from believing these verses. Be specific in how the characteristics would impact your own life.

____

____

____

____

____

IV. Read John 3:17.

To be condemned means to be sentenced to a specific punishment, especially death. A basic tenet of the Christian faith is that we have all sinned (Rom 3:23) and that the punishment for our sin is death (Rom 6:23). Why would anyone think that God sent Jesus to condemn us? In what ways does the person or thing that saves us call attention to the fact that we are condemned—perhaps even seeming to actually condemn us? How do we "condemn ourselves" if the opportunity to be saved is offered freely and clearly to us, yet we fail to take advantage of the chance to be saved?

____

____

____

____

____

Commending God's Works

On any given Sunday morning in any congregation they all sit in the same room, singing the same songs and listening to the same sermon: "seasoned saints" who have walked with the Lord for many years, new believers who are just discovering what life in Christ is all about, and those who are still just curious about the faith or even hostile or angry toward God. Yet somehow, the Holy Spirit works on the hearts of each person present, meeting them right where they are.

If you have already placed faith in Jesus Christ as your Savior and Lord, who shared the good news of this possibility with you? In what way(s) did this person (these people) share with you? Describe the moment when you finally made the decision. If you have not already made such a decision, describe those who have shared the possibility with you and the ways in which they have done so.

Why do you think God chose to spread the news of his love through human beings who already know him? Why is this way particularly effective? Why is it risky?

The Greatest Compassion

Psalm 145:9 says, "The LORD is good to all; he has compassion on all he has made." Certainly God is compassionate in many ways, including by providing the basics we need to live from day to day. But perhaps the greatest example of his compassion is providing a way for us to live with him *now and forever*. A person's eternity starts the moment he or she finds a relationship with God through Jesus Christ his Son.

After meditating on this verse, how might you change the way you begin to share your faith with others? What are some specific ways you might introduce God to others by showing compassion to them?

____

____

____

____

If we are connected to the source of all compassion, it should be evident to those around us. In what areas do you need to be more compassionate? How does this relate to sharing about God's love and the good news of Jesus Christ with others?

____

____

____

____

If someone asked, "If the Lord is good, why do I have so many problems?"
how would you respond? Why?

One More Verse!

When it comes to sharing our faith with others, John 3:16 is important. But if passion is an important element of this process, perhaps we need John 3:17 as well.

In John 3:17, Jesus revealed the heart and motivation of God. When we think about God sending Jesus out of love and the desire to rescue humankind, we should get very excited! Our passion is stirred by the *reason* God sent Jesus. It is much easier and more effective to share our faith with others from a place of love rather than fear. Re-connecting with the One who loves us like no other ignites our passion and reminds us that God chose to redeem and rescue, not abandon and condemn.

Meditate for a few moments on John 3:17, then write down all the words and phrases that come to mind about God and how he has changed your life:

____

____

____

____

____

____

If a friend or family member came to you at this moment and you had the opportunity to share your faith, would you be in the right frame of mind to do so? Why or why not?

What other Bible verses help you re-connect with the source of your passion?

Closing Prayer

Heavenly Father, we thank you for sending your Son, Jesus, into the world to save the world and not to condemn it. We thank you that you are a good King, loving and compassionate. Give us strength and confidence, guiding our thoughts, actions, and words as we share the good news with those you send to us. Thank you for meeting our needs and filling us with your love and compassion for all. In Jesus' name, Amen.∎

L 2

Sharing by Listening

John 4:4–24; Acts 17:16–23

Main Point

By becoming good "spiritual listeners," God will help us to know how and when to share our faith with others.

Background

John 4 tells of a Samaritan woman who came by herself at noon to get water. This was not the usual time to draw water, and rarely would a woman go to the well alone. A good "spiritual listener" might pick up subtle clues that this woman did not want to be noticed and was treated by others as an outcast. As a good spiritual listener, Paul was distressed by what he saw and heard at Athens. He used what he had observed to explain his faith in Jesus. When we are good spiritual listeners, it opens the hearts of those who need to hear the good news of Christ.

Listen and Learn

Think back to a time either in school or at a job when someone really connected with you. You realized over time that you genuinely learned something from this person because you were ready to hear what he or she had to say. How did this happen? Perhaps you feared the person and felt as if you had to listen. Or maybe you sensed that this person was truly making the effort to meet you where you were in life and add something. More than likely it was the latter. When sharing our faith with others, it is imperative to become a good "spiritual listener" and meet them on their turf.

Imagine you are at a friend's house. Your friend does not know Christ, but claims to be a spiritually sensitive person. Secular music is playing, your friend is drinking, and the language being used is very graphic. Out of nowhere your friend says, "I know there's more out there when it comes to spiritual things, but I just don't know what I believe anymore." How would you reply? How would you interject your own story? What types of questions could you ask to keep the conversation going?

I. **Read** John 4:4–18.

Do you think Jesus went to the well for the purpose of trying to strike up a conversation and share the good news with someone—or was he simply thirsty and in need of a drink? Explain.

____

____

____

____

What can this story teach us about using natural opportunities to share God's love with others? What sorts of natural opportunities exist in your own life to share God's love?

____

____

____

____

How did Jesus use the topic at hand—water—to turn the conversation to spiritual things? How did this demonstrate good listening skills?

____

____

____

Do you think Jesus was rude to bring up the woman's history of relationships with men? Why or why not? When (if ever) would it be wise to bring up a person's lifestyle choices when sharing the gospel? Explain.

____

____

____

____

____

II. Read John 4:19–24.

What was the basis for this woman concluding that Jesus was a prophet? Do you think her statement about worship in verse 20 was an attempt to change the subject? Why or why not? What can we learn from the way Jesus guided the discussion back to spiritual things?

____

____

____

____

____

When we are sharing with someone about Christ, how do we know when we have "pushed" hard enough and when it is time to allow the subject to change? Are there hard-and-fast rules or general guidelines, or is it more of a "case-by-case" thing? Explain.

____

____

____

____

____

Why is it important for those to whom we are listening to know about wor-
shiping God "in the Spirit and in truth" (v 24)? How would you describe this
kind of worship?

____

____

____

____

III. Read Acts 17:16–23.

What did Paul notice while he "waited" in Athens? Think about the places
you go where you sometimes have to wait—at the doctor's office, at the tire
shop, in a client's office, etc. What kinds of things do you "see," particularly
with respect to other people, while you are waiting? How can you sharpen
your observation skills for such situations to become better aware of the
people around you and the things they are going through?

____

____

____

Something in the way Paul spoke caused the philosophers in Athens to want to hear more from him. How would Paul's credentials as a learned Pharisee (Acts 22:3) have prepared him for this opportunity to share? What education and/or experience do *you* have that makes you uniquely qualified to share the good news of Jesus Christ in particular situations?

____

____

____

____

How did the opening of Paul's speech at the Areopagus demonstrate that he had, in fact, been a "good listener" during his time in Athens?

____

____

____

____

____

Overcoming Barriers

The story of the woman at the well is well known for many Christians. As Jesus was resting at the well, a woman approached to draw water. Instead of avoiding the woman, Jesus engaged her with a question: "Will you give me a drink?" Not only did Jesus cross social barriers by speaking to a Samaritan woman, he also initiated a conversation by asking a question. Now there was dialogue going. Spiritual listening is much easier when two people are engaged in dialogue.

The conversation that developed was intriguing and a bit mysterious, and it required further dialogue. An important aspect of sharing your faith through awareness and spiritual listening is to keep the conversation open and interesting.

If you were to notice someone who appeared lonely, isolated from family, or perhaps to be from a different country, what types of questions might you ask to start a conversation?

What types of assumptions will you have to let go to become a better spiritual listener?

Every society has social barriers. List at least three social barriers you deal with every day. How can you use the power of observation and spiritual listening as Jesus did to break down those barriers?

Being Aware

Imagine you are in a public place—perhaps the mall, the airport, or a grocery store. As you observe the people around you, what pre-conceived notions might you have? Take inventory of your feelings, being honest with yourself. Are your initial thoughts focused on judgment or compassion? Have you already decided something about these people without knowing their stories? Or are you allowing God to remind you of times in your life when you didn't seem to have it all together either? Explain.

Moving forward, what steps will you take to become a better spiritual listener?

Think about a time in your life when someone affirmed you before sharing a different perspective. How did you react? How did you view that person? Did you feel judged or accepted? Describe the situation.

List three characteristics of the culture around you that you dislike and three characteristics you do like. Why do you feel as you do?

How can you use your cultural dislikes and likes together to create an opportunity to share Christ—affirming what is good and sharing what might be even better?

____

____

____

____

Why is it important to be secure in your identity in Christ before engaging others and their culture?

____

____

____

____

____

Closing Prayer

Dear Lord, we are grateful that you have given us life through Jesus. We desire to share our faith with others by first affirming them and showing them dignity. Teach us to be better spiritual listeners so that we may know how to connect, engage, and share your love with the people in our culture. Open our eyes to see what you see and to lead with love as we share the good news. In Jesus' name, Amen. ∎

L 3

Sharing Your Story

John 9

Main Point

So often, it is our own story that becomes the most powerful tool in sharing Christ with others.

Background

Everyone has a story. You may not think your own story is very important or interesting, but God can use your story to help others. The church often tends to highlight dramatic testimonies and radical conversions. These stories are important and must be shared, but even more "everyday" stories can be effective. Everyday people connect with everyday stories. When Jesus healed a man born blind, the man was committed to telling his story, even in the face of disbelief and hostility. Everyone who is a follower of Christ has a story to share, and it's important to know when and how to share it with others.

If you have a radical conversion story, write out key phrases representing your life before and after Jesus. For example, you might write, "I had no hope and was spiraling out of control. I was hurting myself and others and even though I wanted God in my life, I didn't think he would forgive me. Then, I simply surrendered. My life still has ups and downs, but I have peace and hope now that I have never had before." If your story is not as dramatic or if you grew up knowing Jesus, focus on the kinds of things you *could* worry about but don't have to because of God's help. If you have not yet placed your faith in Jesus Christ, write down your questions, hesitations, or feelings when you consider making such a decision.

I. Read John 9:1–12.

It was common belief in Jesus' day that suffering from a physical ailment such as blindness was "punishment" from God for something you or perhaps your parents had done. How did Jesus correct this line of thinking? In what ways do we tend to assign blame to those who are suffering—for example, "His sin caught up with him" or "Given her risky lifestyle, it was just a matter of time"? How might Jesus respond to this, and why?

What do you make of the particular physical aspects of the way Jesus performed this healing, and why?

How would you summarize this man's "before-and-after" story of his encounter with Jesus? Do we have enough information yet to say whether the man became a follower of Jesus? Why or why not?

II. Read John 9:13–34.

What was the reaction of the Pharisees to this man's healing? What does this tell us about the things that were important to the Pharisees? Who or what did they care about?

Why were the man's parents evasive when questioned about their son's healing? When have you heard people downplay an apparent healing, and for what reasons?

____

____

____

____

____

Jesus had already stated that this man was born blind "so that the works of God might be displayed in him" (v 3). Do you think he was talking about the healing itself, about the man placing his faith in Christ, or about others coming to faith because of what they saw? Does God ever heal people "just to heal them," or is the purpose always to inspire faith? Why do you say so?

____

____

____

____

____

III. Read John 9:35–41.

Jesus asked the man he had just healed, "Do you believe in me?" We are not told of any detailed theological content to the conversation. How do we sometimes "overcomplicate" the idea of sharing our faith with others? In what ways is simplicity the best approach? In your opinion, what are the "basics" that should be included when we are helping someone understand how to have a relationship with God through Jesus Christ?

What do you think was the nature of the worship this man offered to Jesus here? What might it have looked like or involved?

What did Jesus' statement to the Pharisees in verse 41 mean? When we share about Jesus with someone, we have offered sight to this person. Under what set of circumstances would a person not be guilty of sin? What effect does our sharing have on a person's guilt? What does this say about our responsibility when sharing our faith with others?

Effective Sharing

James ran into Tony at their kids' sporting event. "Tony, how are you doing?" James asked. "You look pretty stressed out. Is everything okay?"

"Not really," Tony replied. "I'm spending way too much time at work. I keep telling my wife I'm going to slow down, but it never happens. On top of that, I feel lost when it comes to talking with my kids about God. They've been attending a local youth group, and I just don't know what I think about all that stuff."

"I know *exactly* how you feel!" James said. "Don't worry, Jesus will fix everything. I used to throw myself into my work all the time and didn't have a clue about God. Then something great happened—I got fired! Eventually my wife started making me go to church, and I got some Jesus in my life."

James was ready to share more, but Tony seemed uncomfortable and quickly excused himself.

What are the positive aspects of this story? Why do you say so?

\
\
\

What are the negative aspects of this story? Why do you say so?

\

Where did James go wrong? How would you change what he said and did?

Leaving Room

Although some people are born physically blind, all human beings are born into a world affected by sin and therefore are born spiritually blind. The blind man in the story lived without sight, and Jesus healed him. In doing so, Jesus also revealed to others who could *physically* see that they were spiritually blind and in need of healing.

If the blind man were to tell about Jesus healing him physically, but never shared the spiritual side of his story, then others might have viewed God as a mystical force that can be manipulated into physical healings. Jesus not only meets our physical needs but also our spiritual and emotional needs.

When you listen to someone's story and wonder why God did something like that for this person but not for you, what emotions do you experience? Why?

Jesus answers our questions of faith and also re-directs them to expand our understanding. When sharing your story, others may seek to know *why* something happened or didn't happen. It is important for us to resist giving pat answers for every question, to leave room for the mystery, creativity, and providence of God. How can you be more intentional about this?

Keep It Simple

The Pharisees were trying to figure out how this blind man could now see. As the man was questioned over and over, he tried to make his story as simple as possible for others to understand. It soon became obvious that the Pharisees had already decided it couldn't have happened the way he said.

Personal stories are powerful, but sometimes others have a hard time believing or understanding. Pre-conceived notions and worldviews are stumbling blocks when sharing your story with people who may not be open to the things of God.

Remember, when sharing your faith with others, the response of those listening is not your responsibility. God will use you to plant seeds in others; your job is to simply tell the story.

A good way to start sharing your story is with a "connecting statement"—for example, "I don't know if you will relate to this, but let me share something that made me feel…." What are some other connecting statements you can think of?

When sharing your story, how can you resist the temptation to "solve" someone's problems?

____

____

____

____

When sharing your story, how can you consistently steer the story in God's
direction, emphasizing his goodness and provision?

____

____

____

____

____

Closing Prayer

Heavenly Father, we are so grateful that our stories are sacred and important to you. Help us to learn more about sharing our stories simply
and effectively so that others will be drawn to you and the love you have
for them. Give us supernatural encounters with others whom you have
prepared to hear our stories. Whatever the response, may you be glori-
fied in every word we speak. In the name of Jesus we pray, Amen. ∎

L 4

Sharing by Example

Romans 12:9–21; Colossians 3:1–17

Main Point

The way you carry yourself as a believer is an important part of sharing your faith with others.

Background

One reason people watch other people is to learn. This can be a good thing or a bad thing. If I look up to someone who is a workaholic, loves money, and treats others disrespectfully, I might learn these same traits. If I watch someone who loves God and is always helping others in need in a loving and grace-filled manner, it will leave a powerful but *good* impression on me. Paul made it clear that we should live differently as a powerful example of Christ's rule in our hearts. As believers, someone is always watching us. What kind of example will we set?

First, think of a person who seems to live without the need for God, is self-sufficient, and has worldly values. List five characteristics that describe this person's life:

1. ____

2. ____

3. ____

4. ____

5. ____

Now, think of someone who lives in a relationship with God through Jesus, is an active part of a local church, and does his or her best to put God first in the way he or she lives. List five characteristics that describe this person's life:

1. ____

2. ____

3. ____

4. ____

5. ____

How do your two lists contrast with each other? What general observations
can you make?

Without drawing conclusions or making judgments, are you more likely to
follow one person over the other when it comes to spiritual matters or matters of importance? Why or why not?

I. **Read** Romans 12:9–21.

What are some real-life examples of "insincere" love? Would you rather have someone you care about express dislike for you or continue under the false assumption that he or she likes you? Explain.

____

____

____

____

Paul listed a variety of behaviors and attitudes here that are fitting for those who love God and are devoted to Christ. How would you briefly summarize what he was saying? What makes these attitudes and behaviors consistently possible in the life of a believer?

____

____

____

____

Is it ever possible to "do what is right in the eyes of _everyone_" (v 17, emphasis added)? What was Paul's point here? How do God's standards and expectations inform our efforts to please others? What should we do when God's expectations and the expectations of others are in conflict? Explain.

____

____

How have you seen well-intentioned believers fall because they were "over-come by evil"? What are some practical ways to "overcome evil with good" (v 21) instead?

II. Read Colossians 3:1–11.

When have you faced a difficult task and managed to complete it because you set your mind on the goal or focused on the good things that would result from your completed task? Describe the situation. What are the "things above" Paul was talking about here, and how does focusing on these things help us?

What is the difference between the things Paul listed in verse 5 and the things he listed in verse 8? In what ways might we be tempted to shun the things from the first list but let the things from the second list slide? Are there any sins that tend to be ignored or "minimized" in the church? If so, what are they and why?

____

____

____

____

____

III. Read Colossians 3:12–17.

Where else in Paul's writings did he include a list such as that in verse 12? Where else did he talk about the necessity and supremacy of love as he did here in verse 14? In what ways is love a "binding agent" that undergirds and holds together all that we do as followers of Christ?

____

____

____

____

____

To admonish can be as strong as warning or reprimanding someone firmly, or as mild as advising or urging someone earnestly. Why do we often seem hesitant to do this in the church?

How is it possible to admonish someone "with all wisdom through psalms, hymns, and songs from the Spirit, singing to God with gratitude in your hearts" (v 16)?

What is the importance of all these things in sharing the good news of Jesus Christ by example?

Expressing Gratitude

A good way to set a positive example for others is to begin each day with a heart of gratitude, allowing God to shift your priorities of what's important and what is not important. In God's kingdom, each person can be used by God to reach others. Be realistic about who you are and the need you have for God to work through you. The example you set by living this way will make you a "light" for those in darkness. Your attitudes and actions will become more reflective of God's kingdom, and others will take notice. You will soon be setting a positive example without even knowing it.

What frame of mind is necessary for you to experience gratitude for the good things you have and even for those areas in which you still have needs? What can you do each day to more consistently think in this way?

____

____

____

____

____

____

Strengthening Your Witness

Anger. Rage. Malice. Slander. Filthy language. Paul said to rid ourselves of these things. When you find yourself wrestling in one of these areas, stop and ask yourself why. Don't be discouraged if you struggle. The battle means you are standing against the old ways—and don't forget, God is on your side! Ask him to give you the victory. As you continue to grow as one made alive in Christ, others will notice. You will be powerfully sharing your faith by the example of your life.

Here are some descriptions of God to meditate on as you seek his help in these areas:

- He is our Peace.
- He is our Refuge.
- He is our Strength.
- He is our Rock.
- He is our Redeemer.
- He is our Hope.
- He is our Salvation.
- He is our King.

Which of these descriptions mean the most to you, and why? What other approaches can you take to strengthen your witness as you share by example in the way you live?

Powerful Peace

Because of Jesus we have the incredible opportunity to be born again and have our lives transformed in spectacular ways. Our minds need to be focused on Christ and not on the world.

This is more than just having good thoughts or blocking out bad thoughts. It is a deliberate decision to put into action what we believe. Sharing our faith with others by being a living example is much easier to do if our minds are set on the truth of Christ.

The peace that God offers is of no effect unless we accept the gift and allow it to impact our lives. Before this peace can come in, there are "earthly" things that need to go. Jesus has made it possible for the Holy Spirit to renew your heart and give you a new way of life. The more room that is made in the heart for peace, the more peace will come.

Take inventory. What keeps God's peace from ruling in your heart? What habits, tendencies, temptations, or past issues contribute to this? How can you put your beliefs into action and make more room for God's peace in your life?

____

____

____

____

____

____

Closing Prayer

God of Peace, we are thankful for the way you have shown us that the example of our lives can be a powerful witness for Christ. We ask you to reveal areas where we need to make room for more of you. Rid us of needless worry, anger, and selfishness. We know that true peace comes only from you, Lord. May the peace in our lives draw others to you. In the name of Jesus we pray, Amen. ∎

L5

Sharing in the Struggle

Job 36:15; Romans 5:3; 2 Corinthians 4:7–18

Main Point

Sharing our faith in our struggles and suffering can reveal the real hope we have and help those who are struggling connect with God.

Background

A common question people have about God is why he allows suffering. It is a misconception that Christians have no struggles. The apostle Paul acknowledged the struggles we face in life. Our bodies are fragile as jars of clay, outwardly wasting away, yet God is at work to strengthen and deliver us. Answering the question of why there is suffering by explaining the purpose you have found in your own suffering and struggles will always be honored by God. Undoing the myth that Christians don't struggle can be an effective way of sharing your faith with others when it is done with empathy and discretion.

Think back on your life to a time when you were already walking with God and experienced an incident or season of intense heartache or struggle. Briefly describe the experience, using phrases that honestly express how you felt—for example, "I truly felt like I had no hope" or "I wondered why bad things always happened to good people" or "I was mad at God."

These things honestly represent how you felt at the time. How were you able to get beyond the doubts and discouragement and see the hand of God at work for your good?

I. Read Job 36:15.

The concept of "delivery" here is not like the postal service transporting the mail or FedEx transporting a package. Instead, it has to do with being removed from something bad. If the verse said that God delivers us *from* our suffering, that would seem to indicate an avoidance of suffering entirely— we could just cry out or send up a prayer and God would remove us from the situation. But this verse states that God delivers us *in* our suffering. If the suffering still takes place, then what are we delivered from?

____

____

____

____

The structure of this verse is parallelism, a technique often used in ancient Hebrew poetry; the second line states the same thing as the first using different terms. In what way is the fact that God speaks to us in our affliction the same as God delivering us?

____

____

____

____

II. Read Romans 5:3–5.

Trace out the "chain" Paul described here. How does suffering produce perseverance? How does perseverance produce character? How does character produce hope? Give practical examples if possible.

What do you think it means to "glory" in your sufferings? What is the difference between looking forward to suffering and looking forward to what God will do *through* our suffering? Why is this distinction important?

What is the connection between maintaining our hope and having God's love in our hearts through the Holy Spirit? How does God's love give us hope even during times of suffering?

How do we help others consider that the good things we have are from the hand of God and not simply from our own power, skills, hard work, or resources?

What do you think it means to "carry around in [your] body the death of Jesus" (v 10)? In what way did Paul seem to be linking the suffering of Jesus and our own suffering?

Why is the finality of death so tragic when it comes to the possibility of restoring a broken relationship with someone? What effect should this have on the way we approach our relationships with others, whether or not those people are believers?

How is it possible to "fix your eyes" on something that is not seen? Give some examples.

____

____

____

____

How would you respond to someone who embraced Christianity primarily as a way of avoiding trouble? How would you help this person appreciate the reality of God delivering us *in* our suffering rather than *from* it? How does this understanding prepare us for the "eternal glory" of life with the Lord?

____

____

____

____

God Showed Up

Everyone goes through seasons of struggle and suffering. Comparing our suffering to that of others and trying to assign reason or logic has never satisfied those who seek to understand why suffering is a part of life.

Suffering prevents some people from opening their hearts to God. Christians consistently proclaim the goodness of God, but when the question arises from skeptics about why a good God would allow suffering, believers sometimes struggle to answer. Instead of trying to explain why God allows suffering, it might be wiser to simply share how God has showed up in our own struggles and suffering.

Looking back on your times of suffering or struggle, how have they made you stronger in your relationship with God? How did God change your perspective about life through these seasons?

____

____

____

____

Have you been able to help someone else who has gone through the same type of struggle as you? If so, describe the process. If not, describe how you *might* be able to help such a person.

____

____

____

Sensitive Sharing

Suffering is not necessarily caused by God, but it is used by God to strengthen faith. Although there may be times of struggle and suffering, our hope is secure, and God is with us through it all.

It is important to be sensitive when sharing your faith with others who are suffering. Here are some good points to remember:

- **Circumstances don't matter.** Resist trying to pry for additional details or solve the struggle for others. Your job is to listen, be present, and show empathy.

- **Be patient.** Don't jump in too quickly with your own story. Ask God to show you how and when to share.

- **Never criticize.** People often make bad decisions when scared or confused. Remember that God can turn a bad decision into an opportunity for good.

List three things you feel or experience when someone isn't listening as you try to share something important.

____

____

____

List three things you feel or experience when someone is listening and present with you as you share something important.

____

____

____

Think of a few people who always listen, empathize, and give godly perspective when you are in the midst of a struggle. What characteristics do
you need to work on to become more like them?

How would you summarize Paul's view with respect to our suffering? What is the "bigger picture"?

There are some universal feelings and experiences that are common among people when they experience times of suffering or struggle: fear, frustration, doubt, anger, sadness, loss of control, and asking why. What are some other "universal traits of suffering" God might use to help you strike up conversations, find common ground, and help others who are going through struggles to connect with God?

Closing Prayer

Dear God, we are thankful for the purpose of struggle and pain. Help us to always depend on you when those seasons of life come. Use us to help others see Jesus through their own struggles and pain. Teach us how to share without being judgmental and to walk alongside others without the need to fix them. Use our stories of suffering and times of struggle to bring others closer to you. In Jesus' name we pray, Amen. ■

Sharing from God's Word

John 1:1–14; 3:1–16; 19:16–30

Main Point

Using some "key" verses and passages from God's Word can open up conversations and allow us to share our faith.

Background

Although the Bible can be intimidating, it is still a powerful tool for sharing your faith. God's Word helps us understand that death does not need to have the final say for us; God sent his Son to bring us eternal life. His death on the cross paid the price to make that possible. The Scriptures make this clear; they hold the power of God to transform hearts and minds. Learning how to share this truth is every believer's responsibility. Keeping the process simple and sharing the heart of Jesus through God's Word will provide a bridge to telling others about the hope of eternal life with God.

What are some of your favorite stories or Bible passages and why? What verses from the Bible played a pivotal role in your coming to faith? If you have not yet placed faith in Christ, what Bible verses are you familiar with?

____

____

____

____

Describe a time when someone tried to use the Bible to teach you something. What did you like about that conversation? What *didn't* you like about that conversation? Did you feel closer to God or further away? Why?

____

____

____

____

I. Read John 1:1–14.

If you are already familiar with this passage, try to imagine that you are not. At what point would it start to dawn on you that "the Word" being talked about here is Jesus Christ? What are the implications of Jesus being equated with God, being present "in the beginning" (v 2), and creating all things?

____

____

____

____

Aren't all people "children of God"? What is the sense in which those who believe in the name of Christ become God's children in a different way?

____

____

____

____

What are the implications of Jesus "becoming flesh" and dwelling among us? Why was this necessary? What are the benefits to us?

____

____

____

II. Read John 3:1–16.

Why do you think Nicodemus came to Jesus at night? Was it because he was busy during the day? Was it so he could make the visit in secret? Was it for some other reason? Does the reason even matter? Explain.

____

____

____

____

____

Nicodemus's opening statement to Jesus seemed to indicate that Nicodemus was already beginning to get a view of the kingdom of God. How did Jesus help Nicodemus to sharpen his focus? Why is "being born again" a particularly fitting way to understand God's kingdom and eternal life through Christ?

____

____

____

____

What is the difference between being born of water and being born of the Spirit? By Jesus' analogy in verse 6, what can we say about the work of the Spirit in a person's life before he or she is "born again"?

____

____

What do you think Jesus was saying about the nature of the Spirit? What is the role of the Spirit in a person being born again?

____

____

____

____

John 3:16 is perhaps the most quoted and most memorized verse in all of the Bible. Why do you think this is so? What do these few words tell us about God, humankind, Jesus, and eternal life?

____

____

____

____

III. Read John 19:16–30.

Jesus willingly faced the torture of crucifixion and painful death on a cross. Why? How do these verses link to the passages from John 1 and John 3?

____

____

____

What was "finished" when Jesus died on the cross? The original Greek used the single word *tetelestai* that is translated as "It is finished." In Jesus' day, the word was written on business documents or receipts to indicate that a bill had been paid in full. What was "paid in full" when Jesus died on the cross?

____

____

____

____

____

Why did Jesus have to die? Why couldn't God have dealt with the issue in a way that didn't involve Jesus' death?

____

____

____

____

____

The Importance of Context

There are different ways to share the truth of God, through Jesus, becoming flesh and living among us. A good way to share your faith by using the Bible is to first share a truth and then support that truth with the Scriptures. For example, John 1:14 uses language that is somewhat foreign to most non-believers. Quoting the verse without context might cause the other person to disengage. Providing context could help the other person stay engaged in the dialogue. You might say something such as, "I realize it can be confusing when Christians talk about God the Father, the Son, and the Holy Spirit. I remember wondering myself why God has different names and where Jesus fits into the picture. Then I began to see Bible verses that told the story. When I read John 1:14, I began to see how God came to us at a certain time and in a special way, 'taking on flesh' as we have."

If you used this explanation with a non-believer and that person replied, "Okay, so you're saying that Jesus was actually God?" how would you respond?

In your own words, how would you give context to John 1:14?

Nicodemus's Story

> Even though John 3:16 is familiar to many people—including those outside the church—its meaning may not be clear to everyone. Being familiar with a verse may actually hinder those who are seeking because they confuse their familiarity with comprehension. Until someone knows Jesus personally, the scope and depth of this verse will not resonate in its fullness. The events leading up to Jesus saying these words to Nicodemus are part of a story that people may be able to identify with. The verses after John 3:16 can also provide useful context.

Think of a time in your life when you thought you were in serious trouble for something only to find out it wasn't your fault or it had been forgiven. Describe the experience and the range of emotions you felt.

____

____

____

____

____

Describe the reasons you believe are the cause for non-believers to be turned off when believers try to use Bible verses to evangelize.

____

____

____

How has your understanding of the Bible deepened or "filled out" since you began your journey with Christ? If possible, list specific verses that you now see with greater light.

Helpful Verses

Many non-believers doubt their need for forgiveness. They compare their faults with others and conclude that they aren't as bad as a lot of other people. But even if people believe they don't need God's forgiveness because they are good and moral individuals, there is still something lacking in their lives. This is due to their separation from God, but they don't see it yet. God wants to use you to help others discover that whatever they believe they lack, he will fill.

Always remember that God has been preparing someone's heart in a unique way; our job is to meet that person where he or she is with the tools God has given us. You and I don't save the lost, God does.

What are some additional Bible verses that could serve you well in times of sharing your faith with others? How have these verses helped you in your own walk?

____

____

____

____

Closing Prayer

God, thank you for empowering us to spread the good news of Jesus. Thank you for loving us enough to not only die for us, but also to provide your Word to guide and direct us. Help us to use your Word to draw others to you. Thank you for allowing us the blessing of being able to share the life-giving message of Christ with others by sharing the Word of God. In the name of Jesus we pray, Amen. ■